WASH YOUR LIFE

WALTER THE EDUCATOR

WASH YOUR LIFE

REDUCE STRESS AND ANXIETY WITH THIS POETRY BOOK

Silent King Books a WhichHead Imprint

dedicated to those seeking stress and anxiety reduction

CONTENTS

CONTENTS

CONTENTS

CONTENTS

CONTENTS

WHY I CREATED THIS BOOK?

Poetry can be therapeutic and powerful. Yes, poetry can be a powerful tool to reduce stress and anxiety. Writing or reading poetry allows individuals to express their emotions and thoughts in a creative and cathartic way. It provides an outlet for self-expression, helping to release pent-up emotions and alleviate stress. Poetry also promotes mindfulness and self-reflection, allowing individuals to focus on the present moment and gain a sense of calm. Additionally, reading poetry can evoke emotions and transport individuals to different worlds, offering an escape from daily stressors. Overall, poetry can be a therapeutic and soothing practice for those experiencing stress and anxiety.

CHAPTER

ONE

TRANQUIL PLACE

In a world of chaos and strife,
Where stress and anxiety are rife,
Let me weave a poem, serene and bright,
To calm your soul, like a starry night.

Breathe in deep, release it slow,
Let your worries and fears gently go,
Feel the weight lift from your weary chest,
As peace and tranquility manifest.

Close your eyes, envision a place,
A refuge where worries can't embrace,
A meadow of flowers, soft and sweet,
Where stress and anxiety find retreat.

Listen to the wind as it softly sighs,
Whispering secrets of clear blue skies,

Feel the warmth of the sun's gentle kiss,
As it fills you with pure bliss.
    Let the rhythm of words be your guide,
As they dance in harmony, side by side,
Each syllable a gentle caress,
Easing your mind, relieving distress.
    Inhale the scent of blooming flowers,
Let their fragrance wash away the hours,
Exhale the tension, let it fade,
As tranquility finds its serenade.
    Embrace the stillness within your soul,
As the poem's soothing waves gently roll,
Let go of worries, let go of fear,
For peace and calm are always near.
    So when stress and anxiety are at their peak,
Turn to this poem, let its essence speak,
And find solace in its soothing grace,
As it brings you to a tranquil place.

DEEP INSIDE

In the realm of calm and tranquility,
Where worries dissolve with gentle ease,
I weave a tapestry of soothing words,
To heal your soul, where stress is eased.
   Beneath the shimmering moon's soft light,
Let go of troubles, release the fight,
Embrace the stillness, find your peace,
In this sanctuary, let worries cease.
   Breathe in the fragrance of blooming flowers,
Their petals whispering calming powers,
Feel the gentle breeze against your skin,
As nature's embrace soothes you from within.
   Close your eyes, let your mind unwind,
As melodies of serenity you will find,

In the gentle rustling of leaves, so serene,
A symphony of nature, a soothing dream.
    Embrace the beauty of a starry night,
As worries fade into the twilight,
Feel the weight lifted from your weary soul,
As peace and tranquility take control.
    Let go of thoughts that burden your mind,
And in this moment, true solace find,
For within the depths of your very core,
Resides the strength to heal, to restore.
    So breathe, my friend, and let it all go,
In this sacred space, let your worries flow,
For in the beauty of this peaceful retreat,
You'll find solace, and your heart's rhythm beat.
    In the realm of calm and tranquility,
Where stress and anxiety cease to be,
Embrace this poem, a gentle guide,
To find your serenity, deep inside.

CHAPTER

THREE

FIND YOUR PEACE

In a world of chaos, find your peace,
Where worries fade and anxieties cease.
Amidst the noise, seek a tranquil place,
Where nature's embrace brings solace and grace.
Beneath the shade of a towering tree,
In a meadow blooming with wildflowers free,
Feel the soft breeze whispering in your ear,
As it carries away all your doubts and fear.
Gaze upon the gentle stream that flows,
Its rhythmic melody, a soothing repose,
Let its gentle current wash away your strife,
As it leads you to a calmer, peaceful life.
Embrace the warmth of the golden sun,
As it bathes your soul, one by one,

Let its radiant rays melt away distress,
And fill your heart with serenity and blessedness.
    Listen to the symphony of birds up high,
Their melodies floating through the sky,
Their songs of hope and joy, a healing balm,
That lifts your spirit, like a soothing psalm.
    Observe the dance of vibrant butterflies,
As they flutter, enchanting your weary eyes,
Their delicate grace, a reminder to be light,
To let go of burdens, to take flight.
    Feel the earth beneath your feet, so steady,
As you walk upon the path, slow and ready,
Connect to its grounding energy, profound,
And let it anchor you, safe and sound.
    Breathe in the fragrance of blooming flowers,
Their sweet perfume, like tranquil hours,
Let their beauty awaken your senses within,
And fill your heart with gratitude, again and again.
    In this haven of nature, find your release,
Let go of worries, find your inner peace,
For in the serenity of the natural world,
You'll discover the strength to unfurl.
    So, amidst life's chaos and its demands,
Reconnect with nature, where true solace stands,
And as you embrace its beauty, near and far,
May peace and tranquility be your guiding star.

CHAPTER

FOUR

TENSIONS FADE

In the midst of chaos, find your peace,
A moment of solace, a sweet release.
Close your eyes and let the tension fade,
Breathe in serenity, let worries evade.

Sit in stillness, feel your body unwind,
Let go of troubles that weigh on your mind.
Take a deep breath, let it fill your chest,
Exhale slowly, feel the calm manifest.

Imagine a meadow, bathed in golden light,
Soft grass beneath you, a tranquil sight.
Feel the warmth of the sun upon your face,
As worries and anxieties find no place.

Picture a gentle stream, flowing with grace,
Its soothing whispers, a calming embrace.

Let your thoughts drift away with its gentle flow,
As your mind finds peace, let your stress go.
 Tense your muscles as you breathe in deep,
Hold it for a moment, then slowly release.
Feel the tension melt away, like the setting sun,
As relaxation courses through every inch, every bone.
 Focus on your breath, the rhythm, the sound,
Feel the rise and fall, as you sink into the ground.
Let the weight of the world slowly fade away,
As you drift into tranquility, where worries don't stay.
 With each breath, feel your body let go,
Releasing the stress, letting peace gently flow.
In this moment of stillness, find your sanctuary,
A refuge of calm, a respite from reality.
 Embrace the serenity that resides within,
Let it wash over you, like a gentle wind.
In this relaxation exercise, you'll find,
A haven of peace, to ease your troubled mind.

INHALE DEEPLY AND EXHALE SLOWLY

Inhale the soothing breath of air,
Exhale your worries, let go of despair.
Close your eyes, find a quiet place,
Let the tension fade, at your own pace.
Imagine a meadow, bathed in golden light,
A serene escape, both day and night.
Feel the soft grass beneath your feet,
As worries and stress begin to retreat.
Breathe in the fragrance of flowers in bloom,
Their delicate scent dispels any gloom.
Feel the gentle breeze upon your face,
As it carries away the burdens you chase.
Hear the melody of birds in the trees,

Their sweet song brings you ease.
Let their harmonies fill your mind,
Leaving anxious thoughts behind.
    Visualize a stream, crystal clear,
Flowing gently, calming all fear.
See your worries carried away,
As the water sparkles and plays.
    Inhale deeply, feel your chest rise,
Exhale slowly, releasing all ties.
Let your body sink into the ground,
As peace and tranquility surround.
    Imagine a canopy of stars above,
Guiding you to a place of love.
Feel the weight lift from your soul,
As you surrender to this peaceful stroll.
    In this sanctuary, you are free,
From stress and anxiety that used to be.
Embrace this moment, let it unfold,
As serenity and calmness take hold.
    When you're ready, open your eyes,
Carry this peace as your prize.
Remember this exercise, whenever you're blue,
To find tranquility, within and anew.

MEADOW OF TRANQUILITY

In a meadow of tranquility,
Where worries fade and troubles cease,
Lie down upon the softest ground,
And let your mind find perfect peace.
Close your eyes and feel the breeze,
As it whispers through the trees,
Let go of all that weighs you down,
And let your spirit roam free.
Imagine a field of flowers bright,
Their colors dancing in the light,
Each petal a brushstroke of delight,
Painting a canvas of pure delight.
Breathe in the scent of nature's bloom,
Let it fill your lungs, release the gloom,

As you exhale, let go of all the stress,
Feel it dissipate, feel your soul caress.
   The birds above sing a gentle tune,
Their melody lulls you into a swoon,
Let their sweet song carry you away,
To a place where worries cannot stay.
   The sun shines down, warming your skin,
Its golden rays heal from within,
Feel its warmth spreading through your core,
As it fills you with peace and love galore.
   In this meadow, time stands still,
As you let go of all that ills,
Embrace the serenity that surrounds,
And let your heart be unbound.
   So breathe in deep, exhale with ease,
Embrace the tranquility, let it please,
For in this moment, you are free,
In this meadow of tranquility.

SEVEN

LET YOUR WORRIES FADE

In a meadow, let your worries fade,
As nature's symphony begins to serenade.
Lie down upon the grass so green,
And feel the calmness, serene.

Breathe in the scent of blooming flowers,
As worries disperse, like fleeting hours.
Let the gentle breeze caress your face,
As you find your tranquil, sacred space.

Close your eyes, release the tension,
Feel the weight of stress suspension.
Imagine a stream, flowing clear,
Washing away all doubts and fear.

Listen to the birds, their melodic song,
As they guide you to where you belong.

Let go of thoughts that weigh you down,
And embrace the peace that can be found.
    Feel the warmth of the sun's embrace,
As it soothes your soul with gentle grace.
Allow your mind to wander free,
In this meadow of tranquility.
    As the colors of nature surround,
Let inner turmoil be unwound.
With each breath, feel the calm expand,
As stress and anxiety are unmanned.
    In this meadow, find solace and peace,
As worries and troubles finally cease.
Embrace the beauty of nature's art,
And let serenity heal your heart.

CHAPTER

EIGHT

STRETCH YOUR BODY

In a world of chaos, where worries persist,
There's a secret remedy that shouldn't be missed.
Stretch your body, let your muscles unwind,
A calming ritual for the troubled mind.
   With each gentle reach and soothing bend,
Tensions release, as if on the wind.
From fingertips to toes, let the tension go,
Release the stress, let your worries flow.
   Stretch your arms up towards the sky,
Feel the tightness in your shoulders say goodbye.
Breathe in deeply, let your worries fade,
As you lengthen your spine, feel the calm cascade.
   Stretch your legs, let your worries dissolve,
As you lengthen your hamstrings, let problems evolve.

Feel the tension in your calves gently unwind,
Relieving your stress, leaving tranquility behind.
　　Stretch your neck, release the knots of strain,
Allow the worries to wash away like rain.
With each gentle twist, find a sense of ease,
A moment of respite, a moment of peace.
　　Stretch your back, let the worries unwind,
As you arch and curve, leave anxiety behind.
Feel the flexibility, the freedom to be,
A moment of solace, a moment of glee.
　　In the act of stretching, find solace and grace,
A moment of tranquility, a serene embrace.
Let your body guide you on a journey within,
To a place of calmness, where stress can't begin.
　　So, take a moment each day, and stretch it all out,
Let your worries and anxieties silently shout.
For in the realm of stretching, you'll find relief,
A peaceful sanctuary, a sense of belief.
　　In the gentle movements, find your escape,
From the burdens of life, from the worries that drape.
Stretch your muscles, let the stress subside,
And discover a calmness you'll forever abide.

CHAPTER

NINE

SWEET RELEASE

In the realm of movement, we find solace and peace,
Where stretching muscles grants us sweet release.
When stress and anxiety cloud our minds,
Stretching brings tranquility, a respite we find.

With gentle motions, we unfurl our limbs,
Releasing tension, as worries grow dim.
Each stretch, a symphony of grace and ease,
Unleashing the knots, bringing us to ease.

In the morning's embrace, we rise and we sway,
Stretching our bodies, preparing for the day.
With each elongation, worries dissipate,
As we awaken our spirits, rejuvenate.

Through reaching and bending, we discover the flow,
Our bodies in sync, with each breath we bestow.

We find a rhythm, a harmony untold,
As we stretch our muscles, our spirits unfold.
    In the midst of chaos, we find our retreat,
Stretching our muscles, finding our beat.
Our worries unravel, like threads in the wind,
As we embrace the stillness, from deep within.
    So, let us stretch our bodies, let us unwind,
For in the act of stretching, tranquility we find.
A dance of liberation, a respite from the storm,
Stretching our muscles, our worries transform.
    With each extension, we release the strain,
As stress and anxiety slowly wane.
Through the power of movement, we find our grace,
Stretching our muscles, our worries erase.
    So let us stretch, let us find our reprieve,
In the gentle rhythm, our troubles we leave.
For in the act of stretching, we discover our might,
A sanctuary of peace, in the realm of the night.

CHAPTER

TEN

FIND YOUR RETREAT

In the realm of stretching, let us embark,
To find solace and peace, in every arc.
Let tension unravel, as muscles extend,
A journey of liberation, let's transcend.
    With each gentle stretch, worries dissipate,
As stress and anxiety meet their fate.
The body unwinds, the mind finds repose,
In the rhythm of stretching, our spirit knows.
    Stretch wide your arms, like a bird in flight,
Feel the weight of the world take its flight.
Reach for the heavens, touch the infinite sky,
As the worries and troubles bid their goodbye.
    Stretch your legs, like a river that flows,
Feel the freedom as your worries unfurl and oppose.

Let the tension release, let anxiety subside,
As you merge with the universe, side by side.
   Stretch your back, like a mountain so grand,
Feel the strength and stability at your command.
Let burdens be lifted, let worries be cast,
As you stand tall, worry-free, steadfast.
   Stretch your mind, let thoughts expand,
Explore the vastness of the imagination's land.
In the realm of possibilities, anxiety fades,
As creativity blossoms, in the stretching cascade.
   In the sanctuary of stretching, find your retreat,
A haven of calmness, where worries deplete.
Stretch your body, stretch your soul,
Discover the serenity that makes you whole.
   So let us stretch, with purpose and grace,
In this sacred practice, find our calm space.
Release the tension, let anxiety be set free,
In the embrace of stretching, find tranquility.

WORRIES GENTLY DRIFT AWAY

In the realm of tranquility, where worries cease to be,
There lies a path of solace, a way to set thoughts free.
Stretching the muscles, a ritual of grace,
A dance with liberation, a serene embrace.

With each gentle movement, tension starts to fade,
As stress unravels, like a waning cascade.
The body unfolds, releasing its hold,
And the mind follows suit, its burdens untold.

Stretching like a river, flowing through the veins,
Whispering peace to every cell it attains.
The worries, like feathers, gently drift away,
As muscles untangle, in a symphony of sway.

In this sacred moment, anxiety finds release,

As the body unwinds, it finds a sense of peace.
The breath deepens, the heart beats in tune,
As stretching unlocks treasures, hidden in a cocoon.
    Creativity flourishes, like blooms in the spring,
As the mind is unburdened, it spreads its wings.
Ideas take flight, like birds in the sky,
And worries that linger, gracefully pass by.
    So stretch your muscles, with intention and care,
Let go of the worries, the burdens you bear.
Embrace the liberation, the tranquility it brings,
And let your spirit soar, on stretching's gentle wings.

MINDFUL PAUSE

In the rush of life, take a mindful pause,
A moment to heal, to find inner cause.
Close your eyes, breathe in, and let go,
Release the worries, let your spirit flow.

In the stillness of silence, find your center,
Let the chaos fade, let your soul enter.
Feel the weight of stress slowly unwind,
As you connect with peace, leave troubles behind.

Inhale the calm, exhale the tension,
Embrace the present, with pure intention.
Let your thoughts drift away like a gentle breeze,
As you find solace in the moments of ease.

Notice the sensations, the rhythm of your breath,
As it dances through your body, bringing life and depth.

Feel the beat of your heart, a steady drum,
Reminding you of the strength within to overcome.
Observe the world around, with open eyes,
Appreciate the beauty, beneath the disguise.
Feel the warmth of the sun, the touch of the air,
As nature's embrace reminds you life is fair.
Let go of the past, the worries of tomorrow,
Embrace this moment, free from sorrow.
For in this pause, you'll find the strength to cope,
To rise above the chaos, to find inner hope.
So take a mindful break, whenever you can,
And let the peace within guide your life's plan.
For in these moments of stillness and grace,
You'll find the serenity to conquer any space.

YOUR INNER PEARL

In the chaos of life's relentless race,
Take a pause, a mindful embrace.
Find solace in the present's gentle grace,
And let go of worries without a trace.

Breathe in the calm, release the storm,
Let mindfulness guide and transform.
Amidst the chaos, find your form,
And let the serenity of stillness swarm.

Close your eyes, let your mind unfurl,
Unplug from the whirlwind and the twirl.
Connect with nature, let it heal and swirl,
And find the strength within, your inner pearl.

Feel the earth beneath your feet,
As you surrender to the moment's beat.

Let go of stress, find your retreat,
And let mindfulness guide your life's feat.
    In the stillness, find your light,
Illuminate the darkness, banish the night.
Embrace the peace, let it take flight,
And watch stress and anxiety take their flight.
    Mindfulness, a compass to navigate,
Through life's challenges, it will elate.
In every breath, find a tranquil state,
And let mindful breaks be your steady gait.
    So, when stress and anxiety cloud your way,
Take a moment, let the worries sway.
Connect with the present, let it stay,
And find serenity in each passing day.

FIND SOLACE DEEP

In the depths of chaos, find your peace,
Let your worries and anxieties cease.
Take a moment, just a brief retreat,
To reconnect with your soul's heartbeat.
    Breathe in slowly, let it fill your core,
Exhale gently, release what you bore.
Feel the weight lifting from your chest,
As tension unravels, your mind is at rest.
    Close your eyes, let your thoughts unwind,
Leave behind the troubles that bind.
Embrace the stillness of the present hour,
Let go of the past, release its power.
    In this moment, find your sanctuary,
A place of calmness, a sanctuary airy.

Let the worries drift away like clouds,
As serenity within you shrouds.
   Feel the warmth of the sun on your face,
Or the gentle touch of a breeze's embrace.
Listen to the songs of nature's choir,
Let their melodies lift you higher.
   In this mindful break, find solace deep,
A refuge where your spirit can keep.
Release the stress, release the strain,
And let tranquility in your soul reign.
   For in these moments of quiet reflection,
You'll find strength amidst life's imperfection.
A mindful break, a respite from the fray,
To reduce stress and anxiety, day by day.

CHAPTER

FIFTEEN

BEAUTY THAT SURROUNDS

In the midst of chaos, find your peace,
Release the worries that burden and cease.
Take a moment, a breath, and let it all go,
Embrace the stillness, let your worries flow.
  In this sanctuary of tranquility,
Find solace, find serenity.
Let go of the troubles that cloud your mind,
And in the present moment, true peace you'll find.
  Feel the weight of stress slowly dissolve,
As your thoughts and emotions gently evolve.
Breathe in the calm, exhale the tension,
Embrace the power of mindful intention.
  In this mindful break, find your center,
Let go of anxiety, let it surrender.

Connect with the beauty that surrounds,
And within yourself, true peace is found.
     So take this moment, this pause in time,
To nurture your soul, to let it climb.
Find stillness within, let your worries cease,
For in mindfulness, you'll find lasting peace.

CLOSE YOUR EYES

In the midst of chaos, find your peace,
Release your worries, let them cease.
Take a break, a mindful rest,
And let your soul be truly blessed.
Amidst the noise, seek stillness deep,
Close your eyes, let your spirit leap.
Breathe in calm, exhale the strife,
Embrace the serenity of this life.
Let go of thoughts that weigh you down,
Unburden your mind, let it astound.
Find solace in the present's embrace,
And let anxiety vanish without a trace.
Listen to the whispers of your soul,
As the stress and worries slowly roll.

Feel the rhythm of your beating heart,
And let tranquility become your art.
    In this mindful break, you'll surely find,
That peace and calm are always kind.
So take a moment, let your worries flee,
And bask in the stillness that sets you free.

CHAPTER

SEVENTEEN

STRESS DISSIPATES

In the realm of nature's grace, I tread,
A brisk walk, where tranquility is spread.
With each step, my worries fade away,
As the whispers of the wind lead the way.

Through the emerald meadows, I wander,
Where sunlight dances and colors ponder.
The rustling leaves embrace my soul,
As I embrace the peace they bestow.

The melody of birds, a soothing song,
Guides me through the woods, where I belong.
The scent of blooming flowers fills the air,
Cleansing my mind from all despair.

The rhythm of my steps sets me free,
Unburdened from the chains that used to be.

Anxieties dissolve with every stride,
As nature's healing power becomes my guide.
   With each inhale, the stress dissipates,
Replaced by serenity, I appreciate.
The weight upon my shoulders lightens,
As I immerse myself in the world's wonders.
   The babbling brook, a gentle lullaby,
Cascading waters that never run dry.
I pause to listen, to let my thoughts drift,
To find solace in the moments that uplift.
   The gentle touch of the sun's warm embrace,
Caresses my skin, leaving a trace.
A symphony of calmness, a respite,
From the chaos that once clouded my sight.
   As I walk, stress and anxiety retreat,
Nature's therapy, a balm so sweet.
I find solace in the rhythm of my feet,
In this brisk walk, my worries deplete.
   So let us stroll on this healing trail,
Where stress and anxiety turn pale.
Embrace the beauty that nature bestows,
And let it soothe your heart as it grows.

CHAPTER

EIGHTEEN

BRISK STRIDE

In the early morn, with a brisk stride,
Let worries fade and anxieties subside.
Embrace the healing trail of nature's grace,
And let it soothe your heart at its own pace.
Through winding paths and forest's allure,
Find solace in the stillness, so pure.
Feel the earth beneath your feet, steady and strong,
As you walk, let your worries be gone.
The rustling leaves whisper secrets untold,
As the sunlight weaves a tapestry of gold.
Inhale the scent of blooming flowers,
Let their fragrance wash away the hours.
Birds sing melodies, a symphony so sweet,
Their harmonies bring serenity complete.

As you walk, let their songs fill your soul,
And let tranquility take control.
  Feel the gentle breeze against your skin,
As the world around you begins to spin.
Let the rhythm of your steps align,
With the beating of your heart, divine.
  Each stride is a step towards release,
A chance for your mind to find inner peace.
With every breath, let go of the stress,
And embrace the healing power nature possesses.
  So take that brisk walk, let nature unfold,
As it weaves its magic, untold.
Allow the worries and anxieties to fade away,
And let the beauty of nature guide your way.
  For in the embrace of nature's embrace,
You'll find a sanctuary, a sacred space.
A refuge for your weary mind and soul,
A place where stress and anxiety lose control.
  So walk on, dear wanderer, with a heart open wide,
Let nature be your guide, your solace, your pride.
In the healing trail of nature, find your retreat,
And let it be the remedy, your worries to defeat.

SLOWLY DISSOLVE

In nature's embrace, I find solace deep,
Where worries and anxieties slowly seep.
A brisk walk I take, with each step I tread,
To calm my mind, and lift the weight I dread.
 The sun softly caresses my weary face,
As I wander through nature's gentle grace.
The rustling leaves whisper secrets untold,
And the melodies of birds, a symphony unfold.
 The scent of blooming flowers fills the air,
A fragrance that banishes every care.
The breeze gently kisses my troubled brow,
And carries away the burdens I allow.
 With each stride, my worries start to fade,
As I immerse myself in this heavenly parade.

The rhythm of my footsteps, a soothing sound,
A cadence that brings tranquility profound.
    The vibrant colors of the landscape unfold,
A masterpiece painted by nature's hold.
The greens, the blues, the yellows, and reds,
A palette that soothes and clears my head.
    I walk along the winding path, feeling free,
In awe of the beauty that surrounds me.
The stress and anxiety, they slowly dissolve,
As I find solace in nature's resolve.
    So, when the weight of life becomes too much to bear,
Take a brisk walk, let nature's healing touch repair.
Find peace and tranquility in her loving embrace,
And let go of stress, anxiety, and life's fast-paced race.

REACHING SKYWARD

In nature's loving arms, I find my solace,
Where worries fade and anxieties release.
With each brisk step upon the earth's embrace,
My troubles melt away, finding inner peace.

The healing power of nature's gentle touch,
With every breeze that whispers in my ear,
The rustling leaves, the birdsong's hush,
I feel the burdens lift, my spirit clear.

Through verdant meadows and winding trails,
I walk, letting nature's beauty unfold,
The vibrant colors, the fragrant exhales,
A symphony of peace, a story untold.

The rhythmic beat of my heart finds its pace,
As my feet carry me on this sacred ground,

With each breath, I release, find grace,
As nature's embrace heals, my worries unwound.
    Oh, how the trees sway, like a dance of grace,
Their branches reaching skyward with delight,
They whisper secrets, whispering to embrace,
An ancient wisdom, a calming insight.
    The babbling brooks, so gentle and serene,
Their soothing melody, a lullaby of peace,
I find myself lost in nature's serene,
An antidote to stress, a sweet release.
    So, let us walk, let us immerse,
In nature's wonders, let go of our strife,
For in her arms, we find our universe,
And leave behind the worries of this life.
    Take a brisk walk, let nature be your guide,
For in her embrace, you'll find strength anew,
Let stress and anxiety slowly subside,
And let the tranquility of nature imbue.
    So, walk with purpose, walk with intent,
Let the rhythm of your steps set you free,
In nature's embrace, find solace, content,
And let her healing power wash over thee.

A SYMPHONY OF GIGGLES

In times when stress and anxiety weigh you down,
When life throws curveballs that make you frown,
Seek solace in a remedy that's pure and true,
Embrace the magic that laughter can imbue.

Laughter, a gift that brings joy to the soul,
A medicine that mends and makes you whole,
It lightens burdens and eases the strain,
A melody of mirth that helps you regain.

When worries consume and troubles persist,
Let laughter be the balm that can assist,
For in its embrace, worries scatter and fade,
Leaving room for happiness to be displayed.

With laughter, worries become mere shadows,
As joy shatters the chains that once held you,

It lifts your spirit and sets your heart free,
A symphony of giggles that brings glee.
 So laugh, my friend, in the face of despair,
Let your laughter echo through the air,
For in those moments, stress takes flight,
And anxiety retreats into the night.
 Let laughter be your armor, strong and bright,
A shield that guards you with its gentle light,
Embrace its power, let it heal your soul,
And watch as your worries slowly unfold.
 So let us all gather and share a laugh,
A moment of joy that will forever last,
For in the realms of laughter's sweet domain,
Stress and anxiety shall never reign.

LAUGHTER ON OUR LIPS

In the realm of laughter, stress shall never reign,
A remedy that brings joy, a balm to soothe the pain.
With mirth and glee, let us set our hearts free,
And embrace the power of laughter, for all to see.

Oh, laughter! The sweetest sound that fills the air,
A symphony of happiness, a burden we can bear.
It lightens the load, lifts spirits high,
A magic potion for the soul, as the worries fly.

When anxiety creeps, like shadows in the night,
A hearty laugh can chase away the fright.
It breaks the chains, releases the strain,
And brings a sense of peace, like gentle summer rain.

Let us gather 'round and share moments of delight,
For laughter is contagious, spreading far and wide.

In the company of friends, we find solace and release,
A respite from the chaos, a moment of pure bliss.
Through laughter, we find strength, a bright armor
to wear,
A shield against stress, a light that banishes despair.
It connects us, unites us, in a world so vast,
A language understood, from the first chuckle to the
last.
So let us laugh, with all our might,
In the darkest of times, and the brightest light.
For in the realm of laughter, stress shall never reign,
And anxiety fades, as we find solace in its domain.
Embrace the gift of laughter, let it work its magic
spell,
And watch as worries scatter, like leaves in the wind's
swell.
With joy in our hearts, and laughter on our lips,
We'll conquer the world, as stress and anxiety slips.

FREE AND TRUE MEDICINE

In laughter's realm, a gift of grace,
A balm to soothe the troubled space.
When stress and anxiety weigh you down,
Laughter emerges, a golden crown.

With mirth and joy, it fills the air,
A remedy for worries, a burden to bear.
A medicine that's free and true,
Laughter's power will see you through.

Release the tension, let it go,
With laughter's embrace, let worries flow.
For in its realm, there's solace found,
A sanctuary where peace is crowned.

Let laughter's melody fill your heart,
And watch as stress and anxiety depart.

It lifts the spirits, brings light anew,
Laughter's magic will see you through.
    So gather 'round, let laughter resound,
In its embrace, true healing is found.
Let go of worries, let go of strife,
And embrace the laughter, the gift of life.

LAUGHTER'S MAGIC

In the darkest depths where worries reside,
A gift of grace shall now preside.
Laughter, a remedy for the soul,
To mend the fragments, make us whole.

When burdens weigh heavy on our chest,
And fears entangle us in their quest,
Laughter emerges as a guiding light,
Dispelling shadows, banishing the night.

With mirth and merriment, worries unwind,
Tension released, solace we find.
Laughter's magic, a soothing balm,
A melody that brings us calm.

Let it echo through the corridors of your heart,
A symphony of joy, a work of art.

Embrace its healing touch, let it flow,
And watch your stress and anxiety go.
 For in laughter's embrace, we find release,
A moment of respite, a moment of peace.
Let go of worries, let them slip away,
And let laughter guide you through the day.
 So, embrace this gift, let it be your guide,
Let laughter be your constant tide.
In its embrace, find solace and delight,
And fill your days with joy so bright.

A GIFT DIVINE

In the depths of sorrow's gloom,
Amidst the shadows that consume,
There lies a remedy untold,
A balm for the weary, a heart consoled.
Laughter, dear friend, your healing embrace,
A light that shines in every face,
With every chuckle, every sound,
A tranquil solace can be found.
When stress weighs heavy on your soul,
And anxiety takes its toll,
Release the shackles, let them go,
With laughter's magic, let it flow.
For in the realm of mirth and jest,
A sanctuary, a place of rest,

Where worries fade, and troubles flee,
Laughter's gift sets your spirit free.
　　It lifts the burden, calms the mind,
A gentle breeze, so soft, so kind,
It tickles your heart, makes it soar,
Transforming darkness to light once more.
　　So embrace the laughter, let it ring,
Through valleys, mountains, let it sing,
A symphony of joy, pure and true,
Washing away all that burdens you.
　　Let it echo in your very core,
A constant tide, forevermore,
With every giggle, every cheer,
Banish anxiety, cast out fear.
　　For laughter, my friend, is a gift divine,
A medicine that's yours and mine,
So let it be your guiding light,
And banish stress with all your might.
　　In laughter's arms, find sweet release,
And let your soul be filled with peace,
For in the realm of joy and glee,
Stress and anxiety cease to be.

IVORY KEYS

In the realm of melodies, sweet and serene,
Lies the power to heal, to calm, to redeem.
Notes floating softly on the wings of the air,
A symphony of solace, a tender, gentle prayer.
Strike the chords of a guitar, so mellow and clear,
As the worries and troubles begin to disappear.
Each strum, each pluck, a balm for the soul,
Guiding us to a place where worries don't take their toll.
The piano's ivory keys, soft under your touch,
Unlock emotions, untangle thoughts, and such.
With every delicate stroke, harmonies unfold,
Like a waterfall of peace, the spirit is consoled.
Flutes and violins, their melodies intertwine,
Whispering tales of solace, a soothing lifeline.

Through the ebb and flow of their delicate sway,
Anxiety and stress begin to slowly sway away.
    Let the saxophone's smooth and sultry embrace,
Wrap around you like a warm and tender chase.
Its mellifluous tones, like a soft, gentle breeze,
Sweep away the worries, put the heart at ease.
    Drums beat like a heartbeat, steady and strong,
Driving away restlessness, the worries that throng.
With each rhythmic pulse, tensions start to unwind,
As stress and anxiety are left far behind.
    So let the music play, like a comforting friend,
A refuge from chaos, a balm to transcend.
Let it wash over you, like a soothing rain,
And watch as your stress and anxiety wane.
    For in the realm of melodies, hope does reside,
Playing soothing music, a balm for the inside.
Let it be your solace, your sanctuary, your cure,
And find peace and tranquility that will forever endure.

CHAPTER

TWENTY-SEVEN

MELODIES THAT PLAY

In melodies soft, I find my peace,
When stress and worries begin to cease,
Notes that dance upon the air,
A soothing balm for all despair.

The piano's keys, gentle and kind,
Like whispered secrets, they unwind,
Each stroke of ivory, a tender touch,
Guiding me to a world so much.

The violin weeps, with heartfelt sighs,
Its strings caress, as tears arise,
A melancholy song, yet full of grace,
Tugging at heartstrings in this sacred space.

The flute, a whisper, light and sweet,
A gentle breeze, a lullaby complete,

It carries me away, on wings unseen,
To a realm where serenity convenes.
      And oh, the guitar, with its gentle strums,
Like sunlight peeking through the darkest clouds,
A rhythmic dance, that sets me free,
In its embrace, my soul does flee.
      The harp, a celestial choir of strings,
A symphony of hope and healing it sings,
Its celestial tones, like angel's wings,
Lift me above life's chaotic things.
      So let the music be your sanctuary,
When stress and anxiety threaten to bury,
Find solace in the melodies that play,
And let your worries wash away.
      For in the realm of soothing sound,
A refuge from chaos can be found,
Let the music be your guiding star,
And find tranquility, no matter how far.

ETHEREAL TONES

In the realm of music, find solace and peace,
Let its gentle melodies grant you release,
The strings of a guitar, strummed with care,
Whisper a melody, banishing despair.

The piano keys, a tranquil cascade,
Each note a balm, a healing serenade,
As fingers dance upon the ivory keys,
Troubles dissolve like a gentle breeze.

The flute's ethereal tones, light and clear,
Carry you to a world devoid of fear,
Its melodies float, like birds in flight,
Lifting burdens, bringing calm to the night.

The harp's delicate strings, plucked with grace,
Weave a tapestry of tranquility in space,

Each note a drop of sweet nectar divine,
Easing your mind, like a soothing wine.
    The drums, with their rhythmic beat,
Pound away worries, bringing a retreat,
Their steady pulse, a grounding force,
Guiding you back to a tranquil source.
    And when the day is filled with strife,
Turn to music, let it breathe new life,
For in its melody, you shall find,
A sanctuary for your heart and mind.
    So let the soothing music play,
Let it wash your worries away,
In its embrace, you'll find release,
And anxiety shall find its peace.

WASH OVER YOUR SOUL

In a world of chaos and strife,
Where worries consume our life,
There's a refuge, a gentle balm,
The soothing power of a calming psalm.
The guitar strums with tender grace,
Its melodies a sweet embrace,
Notes cascading, like a summer rain,
Washing away all worry and pain.
The piano, with its ivory keys,
Unveils a realm of tranquil ease,
Fingers dancing, caressing the air,
A symphony of solace, beyond compare.
The flute whispers on a gentle breeze,
Its delicate tones bring inner peace,

A lullaby for the troubled mind,
A respite from the daily grind.
    The harp's ethereal strings entwine,
Creating a melody so divine,
Its celestial vibrations heal the soul,
Making broken hearts once again whole.
    And even the drums, with their rhythmic beat,
Can offer solace, a steady retreat,
With each thump, troubles dissipate,
As stress and anxiety capitulate.
    So let the music wash over your soul,
Let its soothing waves make you whole,
In its embrace, find serenity,
And let go of all that weighs heavily.
    For music holds the power to heal,
To quiet the mind, to help us feel,
A sanctuary for the heart and mind,
Where stress and anxiety are left behind.

MELODIES THAT HEAL

In the realm of melodies, where tranquility dwells,
Where soothing rhythms cast a calming spell,
There lies a sanctuary, a refuge from despair,
Where stress and anxiety find no room to repair.
Let the guitar strum away your worries and woes,
Its gentle strings plucked to ease your soul's throes,
Each note like a whisper, a heartfelt embrace,
Guiding you to serenity, a tranquil space.
The piano, a maestro of solace and grace,
Its keys, like raindrops, softly kiss your face,
With every chord struck, your worries they fade,
Leaving you wrapped in a peaceful cascade.
The flute, a gentle breeze, a breath of fresh air,
Its ethereal tones lifting burdens you bear,

Through its delicate notes, worries dissipate,
As your spirit takes flight, unburdened and elate.
     The harp, a celestial voice, a heavenly tune,
Its strings plucked tenderly, like the light of the moon,
Its melodies wash over you, like a gentle stream,
Carrying away tension, like a forgotten dream.
     And drums, the heartbeat, the rhythm of life,
Their steady pulse banishes stress and strife,
In their primal beats, find solace and release,
As worries are silenced, and inner turmoil finds peace.
     So play these soothing tunes, let music be your guide,
Let it wash away worries, like the ebbing tide,
Find solace and serenity, in melodies that heal,
For music holds the power, to make our spirits feel.

A GARDEN OF POSITIVITY

In the depths of chaos and swirling despair,
Amidst the storm of worry and wear,
One weapon we possess, within our reach,
A beacon of light, a lesson to teach.

Positive thoughts, like rays of the sun,
Can soothe the mind, when worries overrun,
They hold the power to ease the strain,
And wash away stress, like gentle rain.

When anxiety grips, like a vice on our chest,
Positive thoughts offer solace, a much-needed rest,
They whisper of hope, and dreams yet untold,
A balm for the spirit, when it feels cold.

In the darkest of nights, when fears take flight,
Positive thoughts guide us, shining so bright,

They remind us of strength, deep within,
And the resilience that lies beneath our skin.
   With each positive thought, we plant a seed,
Of peace and calm, in this world of need,
They bloom and flourish, spreading their grace,
Filling our hearts, at a steady pace.
   So let us cultivate, in our minds and hearts,
A garden of positivity, where stress departs,
With every breath, let negativity fade,
And embrace the power, that positive thoughts made.
   In the face of adversity, let us stand tall,
Harnessing the energy, when we stumble and fall,
For in the realm of thoughts, we hold the key,
To unlock the door, to a life worry-free.
   So let us choose, in each passing day,
To nurture our thoughts, in a positive way,
And watch as stress and anxiety fade,
Replaced by a serenity, that will never evade.

MENTAL ROOM

In the realm of thoughts, where worries reside,
Lies the power to heal, to let stress subside.
Let's embark on a journey, serene and bright,
To discover the solace of positive light.

In gardens of the mind, we shall sow the seeds,
Nurturing positivity, tending to our needs.
With each thought we plant, with care and grace,
A sanctuary of calm, our minds embrace.

When worries sprout like weeds, threatening to bloom,
We'll pluck them away, creating mental room.
For positive thoughts, like blossoms in spring,
Bring harmony and peace, to our hearts they sing.

In the face of adversity, we'll find our way,
With thoughts that uplift, we'll seize the day.

For every storm that comes, with thunder and rain,
Positive thoughts will guide us, through any pain.
  Like a gentle breeze, they whisper in our ears,
Encouraging us onward, conquering our fears.
They offer strength and courage, when we're feeling weak,
A refuge of tranquility, when life feels bleak.
  With each breath we take, let's inhale the good,
Exhaling negativity, as we know we should.
For in the garden of thoughts, we hold the key,
To a life free from stress and anxiety.
  So let us tend to our minds, with love and care,
Cultivating positivity, a sanctuary rare.
And as we bask in the warmth of hopeful rays,
We'll find solace in each moment, in all our days.
  In the realm of thoughts, where worries reside,
Lies the power to heal, to let stress subside.
Let's nurture our minds, with thoughts pure and kind,
For a life filled with peace, is what we shall find.

GENTLE SAILS

In the depths of darkness, where shadows reside,
Lies an ember of hope, ready to ignite.
Amidst the chaos, where worries collide,
Positive thoughts emerge, like stars shining bright.

Embrace the power they hold, so serene,
For within their essence, lies a soothing stream.
When stress weighs heavy, and anxiety prevails,
Positive thoughts become like gentle sails.

They guide us through storms, with unwavering grace,
Filling our hearts with a comforting embrace.
They whisper of courage, amidst doubt and fear,
And remind us that strength is always near.

With every inhale, let negativity fade,
And let positive thoughts be your serenade.

Let them dance in your mind, like a gentle breeze,
And watch as stress and anxiety find their release.
For in the realm of positivity's embrace,
Lies the key to a tranquil, tranquil space.
So nurture those thoughts, let them bloom and grow,
And watch as stress and anxiety lose their hold.
Embrace the power of positive light,
And let it guide you through darkened nights.
With thoughts that uplift and inspire,
You'll find a life free from stress and its ire.
So let positivity be your guiding star,
And watch as peace and calm are never far.
In the realm of positive thoughts, you'll find,
A sanctuary for your soul, so kind.

UNIVERSE OF GRACE

In the depths of darkness, when shadows are near,
When stress and anxiety cloud the atmosphere,
Seek solace, my friend, in the power of your mind,
For positive thoughts are the light you will find.

In the chaos that swirls, let your thoughts be serene,
Like a gentle breeze that whispers through the scene,
Embrace them as your guiding star in times of distress,
And watch as they lead you to calmness and success.

When worry consumes you, and doubt takes its toll,
Remember, within you, there's a flame to console,
Nurture it with positivity, let it grow bright,
For it will chase away the darkness of the night.

Like a symphony's melody, let your thoughts dance,
Creating a harmony, a soulful romance,

With each positive note, stress will fade away,
And anxiety's grip will slowly decay.
    Believe in yourself, for you hold the key,
To unlock the door to tranquility,
Harness the power of your thoughts, my dear,
And watch as they banish every ounce of fear.
    So, in times of hardship, when life seems unkind,
Close your eyes, let positive thoughts unwind,
For they are your refuge, your anchor, your guide,
Leading you to a place where peace will reside.
    Harness their magic, let them be your shield,
And watch as stress and anxiety yield,
For within your mind, there's a universe of grace,
Where positive thoughts will always find their place.

NURTURE YOUR MIND

In the depths of darkness, where shadows dwell,
A beacon of light, my thoughts will tell,
For in the mind, a refuge I find,
Where stress and anxiety are left behind.
Positive thoughts, like whispers in the night,
Guide me through turmoil, with gentle might,
They bring me peace, they calm my soul,
And help me navigate towards my goal.
When worry creeps and doubt takes hold,
I turn to my thoughts, like stories untold,
They lift me up, they make me strong,
And fill my heart with a soothing song.
In the realm of my mind, I find solace true,
Where positive thoughts, like flowers, grew,

They bloom and flourish, in vibrant array,
Chasing away darkness, with each passing day.
   Believe in yourself, let your thoughts soar high,
They'll carry you through, on wings that defy,
The burdens of stress, the weight of despair,
With positive thoughts, you'll always repair.
   So nurture your mind, with thoughts that uplift,
And watch as your worries begin to drift,
For within your thoughts, lies a universe of grace,
Where stress and anxiety find no place.

BELIEVE IN YOURSELF

In the depth of turmoil, find your light,
Harness the power of thoughts, shining bright.
When stress engulfs, and anxiety burns,
Embrace the serenity that positive thoughts churns.
Let go of worries, let go of fear,
In the realm of thoughts, peace is near.
Breathe in tranquility, exhale the strain,
Let positive thoughts be your soothing rain.
Believe in yourself, in your strength and might,
Banish despair, let your spirit take flight.
With each thought of hope, you'll find release,
And stress and anxiety will find no peace.
Nurture your mind with thoughts that uplift,
Find solace and refuge, a comforting rift.

Embrace the power that lies within,
Positive thoughts, your armor to win.
  In the realm of thoughts, anxiety subsides,
Stress fades away as positivity resides.
So let your mind be a sanctuary of ease,
Where positive thoughts wash away unease.
  Embrace the calmness, let worries escape,
With positive thoughts, find your landscape.
For in the realm of thoughts, you'll find,
A haven of peace, a tranquil mind.

A PEACE OF MIND

In the realms of thoughts, where hope resides,
Lies a haven where stress and worries subside.
When life's storms rage and tempests roar,
Positive thoughts shall be your anchor's core.

Amidst the chaos, seek solace within,
Let positive thoughts be your guiding hymn.
Embrace the power that lies deep within,
To banish anxiety, let the healing begin.

When darkness descends and shadows grow,
Positive thoughts shall cast a radiant glow.
They whisper softly, like a gentle breeze,
Calming the mind, putting it at ease.

In the garden of thoughts, let flowers bloom,
With positivity, fears shall meet their doom.

Nurture your mind with thoughts that uplift,
And watch as stress and anxiety swiftly shift.
    Embrace gratitude, a powerful force,
That brings contentment, a soothing source.
Focus on blessings, big and small,
And watch as stress begins to fall.
    In the tapestry of thoughts, weave joy and peace,
Let negativity and worries forever cease.
For in the realm of positivity's embrace,
Stress and anxiety find no resting place.
    So, dear friend, let positive thoughts abound,
In your heart and mind, let them resound.
For in their embrace, you shall find,
A tranquil haven, a peace of mind.

UNLEASH YOUR WORRIES

n the flurry of life's constant storm,
Where stress and anxiety take their form,
Seek solace in moments of tranquil delight,
To ease the burden, make everything right.

Embrace the calm of a morning dew,
As sunlight dances, painting skies anew,
Breathe in the fragrance of blossoms fair,
Let nature's serenade dissolve your care.

Find respite in the embrace of a friend,
Whose understanding words help mend,
Share laughter, tears, and heartfelt sighs,
And feel the weight of worries slowly untie.

Unleash your worries onto the page,
Through words, find solace and engage,

Let pen and paper be your refuge true,
As your thoughts flow freely, they'll renew.
    In the gentle rhythm of a soothing melody,
Let music's embrace set your spirit free,
Allow its harmonies to wash away the strain,
And tranquility in your heart will remain.
    Dwell in the realm of mindful repose,
Where meditation's balm tenderly bestows,
A sanctuary within, where thoughts can rest,
And anxiety's grip is gently caressed.
    Engage your body, in motion find release,
With every step, let stress decrease,
In the dance of yoga, find strength and grace,
And feel the worries vanish, without a trace.
    In the depths of silence, let your mind wander,
To distant shores where dreams meander,
Where worries dissolve like sand in the tide,
And tranquility becomes your faithful guide.
    Remember, dear soul, stress shall pass,
Like clouds that scatter, leaving naught but glass,
Embrace these moments of peace and calm,
And let your spirit soar, like a soothing balm.

SHARE YOUR BURDENS

In the realm of chaos, where worries reside,
A quest for calmness, let it be our guide.
Seek solace in moments of tranquility,
Let go of stress, embrace serenity.
Embrace the whispers of nature's gentle breeze,
Let it soothe your soul and put your mind at ease.
Amidst the trees and flowers, find your retreat,
Let nature's beauty wash away your defeat.
Lean on the shoulders of friends, kind and true,
Their support will help you see your way through.
Share your burdens, for they will understand,
And lend a helping hand, a steady helping hand.
Put pen to paper, let emotions flow,
Release your thoughts, let your feelings show.

In the realm of words, find your sanctuary,
Let your heart speak, set your spirit free.
Let melodies of music weave their magic spell,
Transporting you to a place where all is well.
Allow the rhythm to wash away your fears,
And let the melodies dry your anxious tears.
In the stillness of meditation, find your peace,
Let worries fade, let tensions release.
Breathe in the present, exhale the past,
Find clarity, tranquility that will last.
Engage in physical activity, let your body move,
Feel the tension melt away, let stress improve.
In the rhythm of motion, find your escape,
Let endorphins flow, a natural landscape.
Allow your mind to wander, to explore,
In the vastness of thoughts, discover more.
Dreams and aspirations, let them take flight,
In the realm of possibilities, find your light.
So, in this journey to reduce stress and anxiety,
Embrace these moments of peace and tranquility.
For in the stillness, the calmness we seek,
We find our strength, our solace, unique.

Walter the Educator is one of the pseudonyms for Walter Anderson. Formally educated in Chemistry, Business, and Education, he is an educator, an author, a diverse entrepreneur, and the son of a disabled war veteran. "Walter the Educator" shares his time between educating and creating. He holds interests and owns several creative projects that entertain, enlighten, enhance, and educate, hoping to inspire and motivate you.